& Wisdom Nuggets For Daily Devotions

DOROTHY V. MCINTOSH

© 2020 Divine Works Publishing, LLC.

Hannah's Secret Weapon to Victory

ALL RIGHTS RESERVED. No part of this publication may be reproduced, stored in a retrieval system, or transmitted in any form or by any means, electronic, mechanical, photocopying, recording or otherwise without the prior permission of the publisher or in accordance with the provisions of the Copyright, Designs, and Patents Act 1988 or under the terms of any license permitting limited copying issued by the Copyright Licensing Agency.

The views expressed in this work are solely those of the author and do not necessarily reflect the views of the publisher, the publisher hereby disclaims any responsibility for them.

ISBN-13: 978-1-949105-17-9 (paperback)
ISBN-13: 978-1-949105-10-0 (eBook)

Published by:
Divine Works Publishing, LLC
Royal Palm Beach, Florida USA

www.DivineWorksPublishing.com
561-990-BOOK (2665)

Contents

Section I.
Discovering Her Faith, Intercession, Forgiveness, and Humility *1*
    Hannah, Who is She?
    Her Story
    Her Covenant with God
    Her Act of Forgiveness
    Her Prayer of Faith
    Her Respect for Spiritual Authority
    Her Prayer of Praise and Thanksgiving

Section II.
Building Relationship, Trust, and Persistence *11*
    Relationship
    Trust
    Persistence
    Contrast Between Hannah and Penninah
    The Secret Place
    Walking in Humility vs. Walking in the Flesh
    Spiritual Warfare

Section III
Enduring Afflictions Builds Godly Character *29*
    Endurance
    Affliction
    Character

Section IV
Wisdom Nuggets for Daily Devotions *(31 Daily Devotionals)* *37*

Questions for Self-Evaluation *71*
Prayer Acronym *73*

About the Author *69*

Foreword

Hannah Secret Weapon to Victory is a compelling story of a woman full of grace and holiness. The humility she exemplified in the midst of her trial is commendable. Her example of devotion to God is a central theme of the book. This story navigates through forgiveness, covenant, faith, and personal spiritual authority. Strong prayer, devotion and trust in God is visible throughout the text.

Dr. McIntosh masterfully reveals how Hannah invokes divine release by abiding in the secret place of the most high God. Endowed with the armor of God Hannah endures spiritual warfare. Her faith was challenged but her Godly character was sharpened. This is an awesome depiction of walking in humility versus walking in the flesh. The lesson learned is to guard the heart. Whatever is going on keep a pure heart. Submission to God through prayer is a prudent factor in spiritual success. The expressions herein can double as motivational moments for leaders. Especially those who seek to make someone else's life better In times of crisis..

The willingness to share this knowledge and experience is indicative of the writer's character. Her intent is to energize you and provide positive connections in the midst of trying situations. The passionate call for effectual prayer to radiate from your spirit is crucial to staying connected. She connects life lessons and prayer to open doors in the spirit realm. This book places the accountability and responsibility of an effective prayer life on the reader. I recommend this book to anyone who desires to master adversity and develop a mature prayer life.

The author concludes with a thirty one (31) day prayer plan that will ultimately shape a powerful prayer strategy in your personal life. This book was certainly written out of experience and trials that have been mastered. The wisdom contained herein is a testament of her personal victory. I am blessed to write this foreword and am humbled to have such an anointed and humble student as a part of class.

Bishop Thomas E. Douglas
Holy Temple Holiness Church of Deliverance, Inc
Lauderhill, Florida 33311

Introduction

On this Christian journey, one must possess a firm belief that whatever God has said in His word, He will indeed do. His word is truth.

The Psalmist declares that no good thing will He withhold from those who walk upright before Him. This was Hannah's conviction. Being thus convicted, Hannah, although under extreme and unquestionable depression, held on to the sure and exceeding precious promises of Jehovah. She purposed in her heart that she would not be moved by the external observation that encroached upon and around her, but by a determined passion that even the heavenly hosts commended and granted approval to her request and her dedication.

Little wonder then, how throughout time, the story of Hannah and her tenacity has been an enduring favorite to both the men and women of God. For without doubt, Hannah stands as a champion amongst those who trust implicitly in the God of our salvation.

Hannah's
Secret Weapon to Victory

Discovering Her
Faith, Intercession, Forgiveness and Humility
Section I

Section I

Discovering Her
Faith, Intercession, Forgiveness, and Humility

Who is Hannah?

      The Bible describes Hannah as a gracious woman, who was favored by God, and whose lifestyle personified true holiness. She understood holiness is what makes God who He is– God! Hannah exemplified a prodigious level of humility and admiration toward Jehovah God. She lived honorably and possessed a deep internal beauty which was signified by her godly character. Her spiritual prowess granted her divine favor with God and initiated the advancement of His kingdom through the obedience of her son, the prophet Samuel. She teaches us all a real life lesson of how one may gain victory through the virtues of humility, wisdom, and perseverance. Though not instant, her prayers remained ceaseless, as she continued to believe and persist until God shut the mouth of her adversary.

Her Story

The first book of Samuel introduces us to the identity of a man from the ancestral lineage of Levi, by the name of Elkanah. He was an Ephrathite who resided in a town called Ramah–within the territory of Ephraim. He was a wealthy and devout man. Two to three times per year, he would go to the worship center at Shiloh, to give sacrificial offerings to the Lord of Hosts and his family accompanied him.

Hannah found herself in a polygamous marriage to Elkanah, which brought about much heartaches as a result of her infertility. She was sorely provoked by her jealous rival, who was productive in fulfilling her husband's desires by giving birth to his sons and daughters. Though Hannah was his primary wife and was blessed, favored, and deeply loved by him, his other wife Peninnah often slated her with intentional merciless ridicules because of her barrenness, causing Hannah anguish and distress. This barrenness sapped Hannah of her exuberance and vitality, leaving her in an unfathomable emotionally despondent state.

The Bible provides no data of Hannah having done any wrong to contribute to her womb being shut up, but it was simply an act of God to remind us that *"we walk by faith, not by sight"* -II Corinthians 5:7. *"But without faith it is impossible to please Him"* -Hebrews 11:6. When we as believers please God the result is fruitfulness! In Hannah's innocence she remained hopeful that Jehovah Jireh (All Providing One) would fill her empty womb, not allowing Peninnah's misconduct to diminish or extinguish her faith.

Hannah was careful to honor her beloved husband and absolutely refused to succumb to the barbaric behavior of her antagonist despite her circumstances. She did not allow her sorrow to leave her at the place where it found her; but rather, she allowed it to drive her to a winning place in life. A place of triumph! She vetoed the thought of becoming a victim because she understood that the exit door from her painful plight was the entrance door to the secret chamber of God in specificity and faith-filled prayer to gain victory. It was a place where the enemy became her footstool and in-turn would celebrate her miracle.

What a great example of faith—complete trust! She never doubted God's power and ability to bless her womb.

Her Act of Forgiveness

The sin of unforgiveness is one of the many strongholds Satan exploits; it is painful and has a limitless course of resentment and retaliation.

It is akin to a deadly poison robbing its victim in a cloak of compromise which precipitates severe repercussions. It is like an acid rain, destroying everything it touches—even the soul. It allows the devil to gain a foothold in one's life, while engaging all forms of ungodly thought patterns inducing torture and subsequent chaos.

Forgiveness, on the other hand, is like a high-powered pressure relief device that flushes toxins and sets at liberty the mind, the spirit, the body and the soul, from the extreme chaotic subjugation orchestrated by the enemy to mentally incarcerate the believer. The eminent effect of forgiveness attracts cleansing and purging of the heart, brokenness in spirit, a sorrowful repentance, and demonstrates purity toward others and more importantly toward Jehovah Roi (All Seeing God). The Psalmist, David declares, *"who shall ascend into the hill of the Lord? Or who stand in His holy place? He that hath clean hands, and a pure heart "* -Psalms 24:3-4a.

Forgiveness is an extremely powerful tool which releases you from expecting to receive retribution from those who have inflicted pain upon you and relinquishes all right to imprison them and to seek personal revenge. Romans 12:17 states, *"Never pay back evil with more evil. Do things in such a way that everyone can see you are honorable."* (NLT). As believers we have not been given the privilege to hold another person's wrongdoing over his/her head, but to forgive without delay as a means to circumvent the manifestations of spiritual muddling and hemorrhaging.

Forgiveness is an all-encompassing undertaking which propels God to impart into us, this most potent gift—the gift of forgiveness. This gift of forgiveness is an antidote to the venomous disease of unforgiveness inspired by the wicked one to thwart a petition from being heard. Prayer that stems from a pure heart enables the believer to penetrate the second realm where principalities demons, powers and wicked spirits operate and rule.

Hannah's situation was difficult, but not without hope. She was excoriated by her rival Peninnah with words that pierced the very core of her soul, but she refused to permit her spiritual pipeline to become clogged with the clutter of this deadly poison called unforgiveness. In other words, Hannah didn't allow her emotions to control her actions. She unequivocally repudiated the enemy's scheme to constipate and block up her bowel of love and compassion because of this conflict. She realized that the enemy's plot was strategic and well thought out, with emphasis to impose the heavy burdens of anguish, distress, and discouragement upon her and hence cripple her faith in God.

The act of releasing forgiveness to her adversary quickly after such ill-treatment was Hannah's immediate course of action. In this regard, she shunned Satan from gaining an advantage over her, for she was not ignorant of his devices.

Forgiveness was embedded in Hannah's DNA and was a vital part of her spiritual chromosomes. Because of this trait, she was not governed by the inherent disorder of unforgiveness which limits the spiritual progression of many believers today.

It is an actual truth, albeit a sad reality that believers in the body of Christ remain in bondage by constantly walking in offense and unforgiveness. It often indicates a hidden hatred that hurts you more than it does the other person. An unforgiving spirit can be destructive, and when nurtured, blocks up one's prayer life. It poisons the believer causing spiteful, vengeful and ungodly actions. This does not reflect the character of Christ.

The writer David declares in Psalms 119:165, *"Great peace have they that love Thy law, nothing shall offend them."* Also in Psalm 66:18, he said, *"If I regard iniquity in my heart, the Lord will not hear me."* Unforgiveness is a serious matter. We must take note of Hannah's disposition and learn life's lesson that true forgiveness is the prerequisite for divine healing and freedom to overcome the most unfavorable circumstances.

Hannah was a most noteworthy example of practical forgiveness. She understood that forgiveness is two-fold; our receiving forgiveness from God is predicated upon us forgiving those who have sinned against us, therefore she swiftly released and let go of any and all assault. St. Matthew 6:12 says, *"And forgive us our trespasses, as we forgive those who trespass against us."* **"The voice of sin may be loud, but the voice of forgiveness is louder. - D. L. Moody.**

Her Covenant with God

The scripture declares in Hebrews 4:16, *"let us therefore come boldly unto the throne of grace, that we may obtain mercy, and find grace to help in time of need."*

Hannah positioned herself in a consecrated place. It was this posture that gave her access into the presence of God-effortlessly. She experienced an overwhelming peace as she entered into covenant with El Shaddai–The All Sufficient God, through the prayer-vow that she made. It was solemn; it was sincere, and it was unselfish. *"And she vowed a vow, and said, O Lord of hosts, if Thou wilt indeed look on the affliction of Thine handmaid, and remember me, and not forget Thine handmaid, but will give Thine handmaid a man child, then I will give him unto the Lord all the days of his life, and there shall no razor come upon his head."* -I Samuel 1:11. KJV.

She pledged to give back to the Lord the son that she petitioned Him for. It was upon this altar of covenant that she gave herself wholly to God; hence, she became worthy of His honor.

Hannah's life demonstrated a high-level of integrity, and evidently, she was a woman of covenant. God loves when His sons and daughters come into a covenant-relationship with Him, with selfless motives as Hannah did. What He did for her is what He would do for all who sincerely seek His kingdom without a self-centered agenda, but with the right vow honoring His Lordship. He is a God of covenant and indeed a covenant-keeping God!

Her Prayer of Faith

Throughout scripture, we find that faith in God is of great significance to answered prayer. The kingdom of God has a standing rule; in Jesus' own words, *"according to your faith, be it unto you,"* -Matthew 9:29. *"For he that cometh to God must believe that He is, and that He is a rewarder of them that diligently seek Him."* -Hebrews 11:6. Therefore, our prayers must not be our own ingenuity but that which is of faith and Spirit-led.

Hannah's hope and confidence did not lie in Elkanah her husband; perhaps he had already broken her heart by his lack of trusting God to open her womb. He was insensitive to dismiss her earnest desire to bear children by asking wasn't he better to her than ten sons. Further, much tension arose in the home because of his apathy toward her primary physical and mental discomfort. She must have pondered in her heart how he engaged the practice of polygamy by marrying a second wife to fulfill his egotism, causing her distress. Elkanah's behavior was unacceptable to Hanna, for she understood unequivocally that her God was the giver of life, the One who waters parched grounds and is the causation of seeds, germinating and generating fruits.

Despite all the discomfort that had driven Hannah to sorrowful tears and loss of appetite; she cultivated an atmosphere for this germination and generation intently. Like many believers today, Hannah's belief system was not broken. She invoked the presence and power of God into her situation by prevailing in the prayer of faith. This powerful prayer tantamount to a grenade in the realm of the spirit. In that moment, the intensification of the presence of God enveloped Hannah and gave her an inner peace that surpassed all human understanding.

The bible states that God's ear is open to the cry of the righteous. He was mindful of Hannah's prayer so He bowed down His ear to her cry—as to incline His ear over the battlements of heaven; to listen to this humble passionate plea of His handmaid.

David said in Psalm 37:4, *"Delight yourself in the Lord; and He will give you the desires of your heart."* Hannah's desire was intense,; she, being a Hebrew woman, longed in her bosom to bear sons and daughters for her beloved husband. Also she wanted to embrace the warmth of her own babies, cherishing and nourishing them and rearing them in the way of the Lord; therefore, she did not release the language of prayer but the spirit of prayer unmasking the bitterness of her soul.

Hannah's prayer was released from such an earnest place of humility and purity. The answer was unhindered and immediate. Her prayer pushed back the darkness and created an environment for the miraculous move of God on her behalf. Hannah knew that faith is an absolute necessity in the life of the believer, *"for whatever is not from faith is sin"* -Romans 14:23.

After Hannah's petition for a son, Elkanah and his family returned to the privacy of their home where Hannah's intimate work, partnered with her faith, made the results evident. God opened her womb. *"Even so faith, if it hath not works, is dead, being alone."* -James 2:17. She conceived and gave birth to the son that she entreated of the Lord while in the Temple of God at Shiloh.

Being in right relationship with God is not a guarantee against the enemy's vicious attacks, but we have assurance in God's word that, *"There hath no temptation taken you but such as is common to man: but God is faithful, who will not suffer you to be tempted above that ye are able; but will with the temptation also make a way to escape, that ye may be able to bear it."* -I Corinthians 10:13. In concert, you have this double assurance that *"No weapon that is formed against thee shall prosper;"* -Isaiah 54:17. Prayer then is a power source that annihilates demonic systems invading your environment and is certainly the choice vehicle God uses to communicate with His people.

God is never impressed with ministerial gifts because they are without repentance; neither is He amazed by sacrificial offerings or intellectual prayer; but untarnished faith and genuine hearts of worship will undoubtedly give access to His throne room where the benefits are plenteous. Faith full prayer breaks and melts your spirit before God and invokes His attention and response. Hannah's prayer of faith forcefully crushed the walls and dismantled the barriers that circumscribed her productivity. Living faith is the essence of life. Hannah's faith transcended the seen plane and became a reality; because faith makes what you hope for–the invisible to become visible.

Her Respect for Spiritual Authority

In our church culture today, respect has been gravely diminished. Eli the priest walked in blatant disobedience to God by allowing his two wicked sons, Hophni and Phinehas, to serve at the temple. It was known to all how they treated the Lord's offering with contempt, showing no regard for their father nor Jehovah God. However, Eli refused to correct them, even after God had instructed him to do so. He was out of touch with God, yet he continued executing his priestly duties. This high-handed, blatant treachery on the part of Eli led to the slaying of his two sons and his own unexpected demise.

As Hannah poured out her soul before the Lord in the temple, Eli observed her lips moving, but her voice was inaudible; so he immediately assumed that she was drunk, and sternly rebuked her by saying, *"put away the wine."* Hannah could have dramatically exited the temple, but despite his lack of discernment, she showed the utmost respect for her spiritual leader. She was serene, polite and reverential in her response. She instantly rejected the thought of taking offense by carefully and respectfully explaining her situation, refuting his allegation. By displaying this godly attitude, Hannah gained uncommon blessings from her spiritual leader, which God honored. This encounter at the Temple was a showdown between Light and darkness.

Having respect for leadership is God-ordained, therefore it is imperative for members/followers alike to show high regard for the spiritual authority whom God has ordained. It is necessary for one's spiritual progress and advancement in the kingdom of God. The experience of Joshua and Moses teaches clearly that for one to be a good leader, one must first learn to be a good follower, and learn to both receive and obey instructions.

Aspiring leaders must recalibrate their nucleus of respect, for many have disrespectfully undermined spiritual authority, and are operating in a spirit of rebellion. This spirit is rampant throughout Christendom across the globe. There must be an awareness in respect to the word of God, to, *"Obey them that have the rule over you, and submit yourselves; for they watch for your souls, as they that must give an account, that they may do it with joy, and not with grief: for that is unprofitable for you"* -Hebrews 13:17. The word obey here also means "respect." Disrespect brings God's judgement, whereas respect brings His blessings and unifies the body.

Her Prayer of Thanksgiving and Praise

And Hannah prayed and said, *"My heart rejoiceth in the Lord, mine horn is exalted in the Lord, my mouth is enlarged over mine enemies; because I rejoice in Thy salvation. The bows of the mighty men are broken, and they that stumbled are girded with strength. The adversaries of the Lord shall be broken to pieces, out of heaven shall He thunders upon them: the Lord shall judge the ends of the earth; and He shall give strength unto His King and exalt the horn of His anointed"* -I Samuel 2:1,4,10. God lifted Hannah's sorrow!

She released pure worship—She glorified the Father
She released pure praise—She glorified the Son
She released thanksgiving in that place—She glorified the Spirit, (God-head Three-In-One)

By: A.L. ALBURY

We should always return to God with hearts of gratitude, thanksgiving and praise worthiness for answered petitions. This was Hannah's response after being granted her request. After her trusting God through her most difficult moments, she was able to dance in the face of the enemy —in celebration of the miraculous victorious power of God displayed in her life. The manifestation of her bundle of joy she received at the hand of the Lord, took her praise, worship and intercessions to new dimensions; and like Mary, Hannah's *"soul did magnify the Lord, and her spirit rejoiced in God her Savior. For He hath regarded the low estate of His handmaiden."* -Luke 1:46-48. *"He turned her mourning into dancing, He put off her sackcloth and girded her with gladness, that her glory sang praise to Him and was not silent"* -Psalm 30:11-12. Hannah was indeed grateful!

*Building
Relationship, Trust, and Persistence
Section II*

Section II

Building
Relationship, Trust, and Persistence

Relationship

According to the dictionary, a relationship can be defined as the way in which two or more persons are connected. The main objective of this connection is that both persons mutually unite in heart and spirit. The idea in the mind of God, when He created man was that man develop an intimate relationship with Him. This idea still stands today. Yes, it is His greatest desire to meet daily with His sons and daughters for pleasurable communion and sweet fellowship. Adam and Eve's faithlessness or tarnished belief destroyed the intimate relationship they once had with God. Ever since, we have seen this same trait throughout humankind where great men and women who once believed God no longer have a relationship with Him and struggle in their faith.

It is evident that in all of God's creation, the element of relationship and its outer-workings is of paramount importance for all and to all creation. To put it simply, relationships are equivalent to the essence of who God is—which is love. All true God-ordained relationships are generated, propelled, and activated by the engine of love. There is no such thing as a hateful relationship. All such relationships are oxymoronic.

We can safely conclude that even throughout the ceaseless ages of eternity, the Creator would have an endless eternal replenishing of relationship in and at various levels. There must therefore be a continuous interfacing and inter-relationship interactions which glorify God in every dimension of the universe. As believers, it is imperative for us to understand and rightly appreciate the function and the foundation of this matter of relationship. To be ignorant of this, is to do oneself a grave spiritual and social injustice.

Trust

Lack of trust in God leaves the believer in a state of wretchedness, struggling to navigate their way through life. One of the many lessons we learn from Hannah is the need for the individual believer to exercise total dependency and absolute surrender—even trust, without borders. Far too many believers settle with the notion that this matter of trust is just a matter of believing in God. On the contrary, like Hannah, who gave God her all, we too must—when we come to God—give Him our all and in all. For He will have it all or none at all. Trust then is the heaven born currency by which our relationship with God flows unimpeded in the stream of eternal life. Read Ezekiel 47.

It is for this reason, that our Savior admonishes us to be like little children when it comes to the matter of trust. He insists that we become childlike, not childish. As a child trusts his earthly father, so are we to trust our heavenly father; with great simplicity and abundant soundness.

In His inaugural address concerning His kingdom, our Savior defines for us what it means to trust our heavenly Father. He calls our attention to Matthew 5:26-29, *"Behold the fowls of the air: for they sow not, neither do they reap, nor gather into barns; yet our heavenly Father provides for them."* He goes further and says, *"consider the lilies of the field, how they grow; they toil not, neither do they spin: and even Solomon in all his glory was not arrayed like one of these."* And then, as if to make the assurance triple sure, Jesus gave a third and powerful illustration concerning trust. He said to His audience and to us today, *"Or what man is there of you, whom if his son asks for bread, will he give him a stone? Or if he asks a fish, will he give him a serpent? If ye then being evil, know how to give good gifts unto your children, how much more shall your heavenly Father which is in heaven give good things to them that asks Him?"* -Matthew 7:9-11.

So the lesson is that we can trust our heavenly Father, for He is more than willing, yea anxious, to give us what we need as we lay our trust in Him. It is imperative therefore, that every present truth fertilizes and cultivates the field of trust, to do otherwise is to our heavenly Father an act of doubt and spiritual treason. Doubt is the opposite of faith; it causes you to live a life of uncertainty. It also causes you to question the integrity and character of God, which makes it a damnable sin.

We know that every soldier in the army of the Lord goes forward and must follow his General's instructions and directions if he is to be a true soldier in the army of the Lord. We can better appreciate the hymn writer John H. Sammis' admonition as found in that old christian song, "Trust and obey, for there's no other way, to be happy in Jesus, but to trust and obey."

Trust then, in the christian sphere, is synonymous with blessedness. A state of continual awareness of and appreciation for the presence of the Eternal One—as is demonstrated in the life of the three Hebrew worthies, and the aged prophet Daniel. No amount of external intimidation, threats, or promises of reward or favor could deter any of these Hebrews from an abiding trust in the God of Israel. These three young men would rather die, even burn than to lose trust in Jehovah God. Daniel would rather face hungry lions in a den than to surrender trust in the Lord his God. Selah!

Persistence

For the believer, persistence in prayer is more than just an essential element, it is a God required commandment to all. As illustrated in Luke 18, our Savior took the time to demonstrate the powerful results of persistence. Hear the gospel writer, *"And He spake a parable unto them to this end, that men ought always to pray and not to faint."* -Luke 18:1, for a brief moment let the reader analyze this profound lesson as told by the Savior in this parable. This poor widow was powerful in persisting that this unjust judge give audience to her concerns. We can almost imagine the Savior with the joyful question, *"And shall not God avenge his own elect, which cry day and night unto Him, though He bears long with them?"*

The lesson specifically was to point the believer in the opposite direction that fainting, or giving up, or failing to continue is not to be a part of the christian experience in the matter of prayer. This same thought is described when our Lord retaught it to the inquiring disciple, "no man having put his hand to the plough, and looking back, is fit for the kingdom of God." In other words, its persistence (in prayer or in life) or dismissal. Faith full persistent prayer brings blessings and that more abundantly.

A powerful typical illustration concerning these three, God required agencies, in the life of the Christian, (Relationship, Trust and Persistence) is found in I Corinthians 13:13 where the great Apostle Paul declares, *"Now abideth faith, hope, charity, these three, but the greatest of these is charity."* But for us today the anti-typical is "Now abideth these three, Relationship, Trust and Persistence, but the greatest of these three, because it intertwines and interconnects and lays the foundation for the other two is Persistence.

A commonly used synonym for the word persistence in the days of the Apostle Paul is found in I Corinthians 14:1, where the Apostle admonishes the believer to earnestly pursue, persevere, follow after and be persistent in love. The believer then has no other option when it comes to persistency in whatever life experience arena (prayer, exercising of faith, maintaining servant relationship with God, and to hold fast the throttle of heaven's upward moving train as it locomotions progress from earth to glory).

Just one chapter back. Chapter 13 of I Corinthians the Apostle Paul delineates with clear cutting illustration, the power of persistence with respect to love. Love never gives up, love never fails.

Contrast Between Hannah and Penninah

HANNAH	PENINNAH
Loving	Cruel
Compassionate	Antagonistic
Kind	Passionless
Humble	Prideful
Reserved	Inconsiderate
Wise	Unwise
Peaceful	Contentious
Optimistic	Pessimistic
Respectful	Insolent
Prayerful	Irreverent

The Secret Place

"Embracing the stillness of God; invoking divine release."

Hannah experienced a moment of truth while in the midst of a challenging situation. She received a divine revelation that her status was a temporary one and was subject to change. With this renewed perspective and with a buoyant spirit, Hannah was transported from a state of indifference to one of elasticity and ebullience.

Her resolve to enter into the Most Holy Place at the Temple of God was strategic. To demonstrate her obedience to God, she went to the physical altar where the presence of God resided. Let it be resolved that long before Hannah made her trek to Shiloh on this occasion, "the secret place of the most High God was already in her heart."

It is incumbent therefore to ensure that this "secret place" is established in the daily lives of believers, as they make consecration, daily dedication and daily devotion on the altar of sacrifice. Hannah did not go to Shiloh to seek God, she took God with her. As the Savior with His discourse with the woman at the well said, *"the time is coming when ye shall neither in this mountain, nor yet in Jerusalem, worship the Father."* St. John 4:21. The presence of God is not limited by time, space, or location. This resolution heightened Hannah's effectiveness in defeating the taunting insults of the enemy which had been designed to break her spirit and engender oppressiveness. Her decision was one of divine origin coupled with divine mystery. This decision was carefully designed to annihilate the enemy's plan, and at the same time empower the handmaiden of God to pursue the path of trust and to hold the hand of infinite love by the power of faith. Victory was inevitable.

The secret place is not just a physical quiet place, but it is an inner sanctuary that hosts the presence of God. It is a restricted area of purity and serenity. It represents the Holy of Holies; a consecrated place that wards off offenses, worries and bitterness, and prohibits all forms of impurities. This inner haven alludes to the heart, that secret place, which must be kept consecrated and protected at all times. Why? The bible says that, *"The heart is deceitful above all things, and desperately wicked: who can know it?"* -Jeremiah 17:9a KJV. The wise man Solomon said, *"Keep (Guard) your heart with all diligence, for out of it are (flows) the issues of life."* -Proverbs 4:23.

It is incumbent upon believers today, not only in times of testing, but on a day-to-day basis to resort to the secret place of the Most High for guidance and help even in times of need. It must be constant; it must be ceaseless. God desires lasting relationships; therefore it is equally required to maintain an intimate relationship with the Father, even as Jesus did when He walked upon the earth. It is for that reason He declared in His hour of temptation that, *"Man shall not live by bread alone, but by every word that proceedeth out of the mouth of God."* -St. Matthew 4:4. KJV. To Him it was a matter of life. He further stated in St. John 6:53 & 56, *"Except ye eat the flesh of the Son of man, and drink His blood, ye have no life in you." "He that eateth my flesh, and drinketh my blood, dwelleth in me, and I in him."* KJV. He is speaking of perpetual intimacy.

The record is clear in St. Luke 5:16, "But Jesus often withdrew to lonely places and prayed." NIV. These were essential places of silence and solitude. You must endeavor daily to position yourselves on the altar where the natural encounters the supernatural and divine revelation is imparted. It is a place where your heart connects to the heart of God and your ears are in-tuned to hear what the Spirit would say unto His church. This is the all-encompassing spirit-filled, life-giving, revitalizing and impartation of divine power. Become wired to that ultimate power in the universe, Holy Spirit Himself, and build a habitation for the high-frequency of His power to flow in and through your life. "He that dwelleth in the secret place of the Most High shall abide under the shadow of the Almighty." Psalm 91:1. KJV.

Live–dwell–reside–abide–in the secret place of prayer. When your all is submitted on the altar, that secret place, there will be an emergence of the character and full development of Christ in your life. Dreams will be realized, visions will be discovered, destiny will manifest and purpose will become a reality. Live in proximity with the Lover of your Soul by intimate relations that's sacred and solemn. *"To be a Christian without prayer is no more possible than to be alive without breathing."* - Martin Luther.

Walking in Humility vs. Walking in the Flesh

"True humility is not thinking less of yourself; it is thinking of yourself less." C. S. Lewis.

The Apostle Peter admonishes us to, "be clothed with humility." I Peter 5:5. In essence he was saying that humility ought to be the believer's dress-code, indeed covering. Humbling your life before God involves a total submission of heart, mind, spirit, body, will and emotion. This was demonstrated by our Savior, who showed the greatest example of humility.

Philippians 2:6-8 says, "Who being in the form of God, thought it not robbery to be equal with God: But made himself of no reputation, and took upon him the form of a servant, and was made in the likeness of men. And being found in fashion as a man, He humbled himself, and became obedient unto death, even the death of the cross." He totally abandoned the flesh subjecting Himself to a sinners death, proving to be the source of true humility.

Humility then is bare-faced and has absolutely no hidden agenda. It reflects a lifestyle of purity of one's heart and thoughts. It is defined as being modest, (having a lesser view of one's own significance), therefore, it should never be misconceived as a sign of weakness. Far too often and far too many often confuse meekness (humility) with weakness. Let us be clear. The bible states that Moses was the meekest man on earth, yet the record shows that Moses was strong, firm, ready to battle in the name of Jehovah. No weakling intercedes on behalf of an entire nation and prevails. No weakling could receive such commendation from Jehovah when He said of Moses, *"I know him," "I speak to him face to face."* The scripture says, *"the meek shall inherit the earth."* **Humility then is a power well-controlled and governed by the impulses of the Spirit of Truth.** Bearing this in mind, one can conclusively say that humility presents a powerful defensive weapon that guards one's life against the contrary affections and lusts of the flesh.

The flesh represents the sinful nature and desires of man. It must not be allowed to give birth to sin, but be put to death on a daily basis. The word of God specifically instructs the believer not to walk in accordance with the dictates of the flesh, but that of the spirit of God. Hence, the Apostle admonishes all believers to:

1. Mortify the deeds of the body. Romans 8:13.
2. Present your bodies a living sacrifice, holy, acceptable unto God... Romans 12:1.
3. I am crucified with Christ: nevertheless I live; yet not I, but Christ liveth in me: Galatians 2:20.
4. I die daily. I Corinthians 15:31.

Galatians 5:16 declares, *"This I say then, Walk in the Spirit, and ye shall not fulfill (gratify) the lust (desires) of the flesh."*

Being clothed with humility therefore is of significant importance in the believer's life. The spirit of humility repudiates the works of the flesh, hence, creates an atmosphere of tranquility from which the glory of God emanates. Humility drives the believer to his/her knees engaging the spiritual disciplines of prayer and fasting. Humility constitutes power.

It was the prophet Micah, who centuries before the Savior came, gave a precise and clear-cut pattern of what God requires of all men during this time of earth's history. Hear the prophet speak in Micah 6:8, *"He hath shewed thee, O man what is good; and what doth the Lord require of thee, but to do justly, to love mercy, and to walk humbly with thy God?"*

Walking humbly with God is the consummate demonstration of a life filled with the spirit of God. It is within this category-the spirit of humility, that the Psalmist rejoice-fully declares in chapter 119:165, "Great peace have they that love Thy law, nothing, absolutely nothing shall offend them." Perhaps the most clear-cut account of practical humility in the life of the early christian church is documented for us in I Corinthians 6:7, *"Now therefore there is utterly a fault among you, because ye go to law one with another. Why do ye not rather take wrong? Why do ye not rather suffer yourselves to be defrauded?"* This is the epitome of humility!

Every true believer knows that the works of the flesh are diametrically opposed to that of the spirit. The scriptures leave no occasion for doubt as to what the works of the flesh are.

Galatians 5:19-21 declares, *"Now the works of the flesh are manifest, which are these; adultery (violation of the marital bed), fornication, uncleanness (moral impurity), lasciviousness, idolatry (idol worship), witchcraft (the aid of evil spirits to manipulate), hatred (extreme disdain), variance, emulations, wrath, strife, seditions, heresies, envying, murders, drunkenness, revelings, and such like".*

I Peter 4:3 says, *"For the time past of our lives may suffice us to have wrought the will of the Gentiles, when we walked in lasciviousness, lusts, excess of wine, revelings, banqueting, and abominable idolatries:".*

Romans 1:18-25 declares, "For the wrath of God is revealed from heaven against all ungodliness and unrighteousness of men, who hold the truth in unrighteousness; Because that which may be known of God is manifest in them; for God hath shewed it unto them. For the invisible things of him from the creation of the world are clearly seen, being understood by the things that are made, even His eternal power and Godhead; so that they are without excuse:

Because that, when they knew God, they glorified him not as God, neither were thankful; but became vain in their imaginations, and their foolish heart was darkened. Professing themselves to be wise, they became fools, and changed the glory of the incorruptible God into an image made like to corruptible man, and to birds, and four-footed beasts, and creeping things. Wherefore God also gave them up to uncleanness through the lusts of their own hearts, to dishonor their own bodies between themselves: Who changed the truth of God into a lie, and worshipped and served the creature more than the Creator, who is blessed for ever. Amen." These are all illustrations of the works of the flesh.

The sad reality is that the works of the flesh are about the natural outworking of a life devoid of and separated from God; example, it is as natural as breathing air for a man to proposition the opposite sex in and at every occasion he can. Only the spirit of God controlling the reins of the heart can resist the natural human tendency to fulfill the lust of the flesh. *"For the flesh lusted against the Spirit, and the Spirit against the flesh: and these are contrary the one to the other:"* -Galatians 5:17.

Neither does it leave any doubt as to what the work/fruit of the Spirit are: Galatians 5:22-24 declares, *"But the fruit of the Spirit is love, joy, peace, long-suffering, gentleness, goodness, faith, meekness, temperance: against such there is no law. And they that are Christ's have crucified the flesh with the affections and lusts."*

Walking in the spirit of humility then results in ultimate victory over the works of the flesh.

Spiritual Warfare

Why do believers complain when faced with a test? Once you accept Jesus as Lord of your life, you automatically enlist in spiritual warfare. The great Apostle Paul admonishes the children of God that the secret to comprehending the armor of God is to *"be strengthened with might by His Spirit in your inner man;"* and to *"be strong in the Lord and in the power of His might."* In other words, one must be fortified in the Word of God to be able to overcome the diabolical assignments of the enemy against one's life.

He further admonishes the believer, to, *"put on the whole armor of God, that ye may be able to stand against the wiles (tricks, schemes, strategies) of the devil."* -Ephesians 6:11. These strategies are intended to ensnare, entrap and deceive the believer. In that case, the believer should then be fully clad with the complete armor of God to engage in this spiritual warfare. As we dress ourselves daily in this armor, we are able to keep Satan at bay.

This wrestling is not in the natural but in the spiritual realm, therefore, you must rid yourselves of every secret sin and natural tendencies and human frailties, and draw strength from Holy Spirit through intimate worship, in order to be effective in this engagement. The armor belongs to God and has been given to the believer as a defensive and an offensive weapon against the adversary of your soul.

The articles that comprise this heaven ordained Armour are these:

The Belt of Truth

The belt of truth fastened around the waist (loins) signifies one having the moral courage to stand in truth against all wrong.

"God desires truth in the inward parts:" Psalm 51:6.

The believer must be established in truth and sincerity, with our motives being that of purity. When the armor of truth becomes a discipline in your life, the cloak of compromise will be obliterated. This belt of truth is very crucial in protecting the believer against the lies of the evil one. This Belt of Truth is like gorilla glue keeping all the articles intact.

Living outside of truth makes the other articles invalid, inoperable. Living outside of truth also renders the believer impotent and easily overcome. Hence, the Savior statement concerning the power of truth, "and ye shall know the truth, the truth shall make you free." St. John 8:32. We can therefore conclude that truth brings freedom, lies equal to bondage and death.

The belt of truth, worn daily by the believer, reflects the purity of the heart and mind, which involves our conversations /words, our behavior/actions. Let the believer therefore arise and gird himself with this powerful article as we face the enemies of our souls. Being ever conscious of that long time aged admonition that comes down through the ages as the scriptures speak to us by Moses, "Keep thee far from a false matter, and the innocent and righteous slay thou not:" Exodus 23:7.

The Breastplate of Righteousness

This article signifies one having uprightness of heart; standing firm against lawlessness; always pursuing the will of God; living in accordance with the principles of His Word.

The breastplate is an essential article that heavily shields and protects the heart cavity. Its purpose is for the believer's survival in spiritual warfare; therefore when the believer's heart is upright, no deadly toxin such as (unforgiveness, bitterness, envy, resentment, hatred) can penetrate.

In the natural the heart is that life-giving organ that supplies the necessary nutrients, via the bloodstream to all parts of the body. It is important therefore that as in the natural, so in the spiritual, our hearts ought to be sanctified, purified, thus supplying all the spiritual nutrients necessary for the growth and development of the soul.

A weakened heart correlates to a weak and vacillating organism/body. It is incumbent therefore that our hearts be closely guarded, indeed covered with the breastplate of righteousness.

Feet Shod with the Preparation of the Gospel of Peace

Equipped with foot-gears that are firm and stable to engage the enemy; being in a state of readiness prompted by the gospel of peace.

This readiness to go wherever duty calls is the vehicle that the Master General has chosen for all of His foot soldiers. Every soldier then is at best a mobile gospel carrying individual, whether they're moving on the land, or by sea or by air.

The gospel then is not to be restricted by any barrier or obstruction that the enemy might initiate in the conflict. We are constantly on the move as clearly illustrated in the short gospel of Mark. The most descriptive word used concerning our Lord's actions in His ministry is the word straightway, which tells us that Jesus was constantly on the move from one miracle to the next, from one parable to the next, from one location to the next.

This lesson that the Apostle Paul presented to us here was long foreshadowed in the words of the gospel Prophet Isaiah and the Prophet Nahum, *"Behold upon the mountains the feet of him that bringeth good tidings, that publisheth peace;"* *"And let us run with patience the race that is set before us."* -Hebrews 12:1.

Note with care that this article also involves the element of peace. In His inaugural address on the state of His kingdom, the Master declared, *"blessed are the peacemakers: for they shall be called the children of God."* -Matthew 5:9. In all of our battles, therefore, and all our conflicts, we are instructed to *"let the peace of God rule in our hearts."* -Colossians 3:15.

The Shield of Faith

This article you would note in proportion to the size of all the others is larger than the others and is designed to cover the entire body. It is known as an extinguisher.

It must be strong above every other article and must always be raised high to safeguard, protect, defend and extinguish the "fiery arrows" and lies thrown by the enemy. In addition, the lesson is, our faith must be looming, overspreading our entire walk with the Lord. Further, it bears emphasizing that this shield of faith is an active, ever moving, ever growing, ever increasing article in the Christian armoury.

Thus, to the often asked question, how is one to grow in faith? The answer comes back in the resounding clash, *"faith cometh by hearing and hearing by the word of God,"* which is to say, to increase one's faith is to increase one's hearing, reading, studying, prayerfully meditating, actively assimilating (taking in fully) the word of God. Little appreciation towards the word of God translates into little faith in God. To be devoid of exercising this article, renders the warrior vulnerable to destruction at any time and in any place. Thus, we are told to *"walk by faith and not by sight"* -II Corinthians 5:7.

We are required by scripture to have a sound understanding of the value of faith. Little wonder then, that the Apostle Paul delineates for us by an entire chapter, Hebrews 11, the value and the consequences of exercising this article. As a matter of fact, he lays emphasis on the word "understand" in regard to faith. *"Through faith we understand that the worlds were framed by the word of God, so that things which are seen were not made of things which do appear."* -Hebrews 11:3. Faith then is that vehicle that moves the believer into the atmosphere of the acceptance of God. *"But without faith it is impossible to please God."* -Hebrews 11:6.

From the early account in the book of Genesis, we are told that Adam had face-to-face communication with his Maker. Faith was not at that time prosecuted, however, since the entrance of sin, faith became a heaven ordained requirement in the plan of salvation, hence the Apostle tells us, by faith Abel and all the patriarchs, prophets and all the righteous men of antiquity drove the vehicle of faith in their walk with God. Whether it was an act of worship, or offering of sacrifice, or simply obeying the express word of Jehovah, the ancients were all moved by faith. Faith then is a natural antidote for sin. Faith cancels out suffocates sin. Sin is doubt, faith is belief. Faith is life, sin is death. Faith is the shield that quenches every fiery dart of the enemy.

The Helmet of Salvation

This article, the helmet is used to protect the center of reason and will power, for it is here that decisions are made, for or against-for God which leads to salvation, or against the enemy which leads to victory. The helmet is therefore a saving device and must be worn at all times. Selah!

No true warrior engages the battle without his helmet. For he must fight the good fight of faith with all his wits and spiritual prowess. The battlefield is the mind. The forces that are arrayed against the warrior makes their attack on this mental spiritual battlefield. Therefore, the Christian's mind is a primary object in which the enemy seeks to establish the smallest yea minutest foothold and thus engage the spiritual conflicts that could unsettle the warrior and cause him to stumble. Our Savior gave a perfect illustration of this in His own conflicts with the enemy when He said with confidence, *"for the prince of this world cometh, and hath nothing in me."* -St. John 14:30. The Lord was saying, that wicked spirit the prince of devils could find no entry points in his mind to confuse or confound Him.

Like the heart, (inspiration tells us to guard well the avenues of the soul, or as the wise man said, keep your heart with all diligence for out of it are the issues of life). The mind too must be protected, constantly guarded, always alert and held in check by this article-this helmet of salvation. Again here the battle is won or lost. *"For as he thinketh in his heart, so is he:"* To put it in a more modern vernacular, Elbert Hubbard says, *"man is not what he thinks he is, but what he thinks, he is"*.

The Sword of the Spirit - represents the Word of God.

It is the most powerful weapon (ammunition) used to pierce and penetrate the darkness and evil intrusions believer's face today. One must immerse himself in the word of God daily, to make this fight worthwhile. It is with this view in mind that the word of God declares in Joshua 1:7-9. This is a daily undertaking. It is with this weapon that the Savior was able to defeat the enemy in the wilderness of temptation. With every attack thrown at the Savior, He raised His sword and responded, *"It is written…"* It is also to know that even the enemy was well versed in scripture, for on this occasion he attacked the Savior with the word, though it was misapplied.

It is for this reason that the child of God is instructed to *"rightly divide the word of truth."* -II Timothy 2:15. This sword of the spirit is the most crucial part of the spiritual armor, for it is of the entire armory the only offensive article in the entire armory. The scripture refers to it as a "double-edged sword." It is here that perhaps we should delve a little deeper into the expression. "double-edged sword." While it is true as stated above that this sword of the Spirit is the only offensive article in this christian armory, it is equally true that the sword is also a defensive device, hence the scripture designation double-edged sword.

The reference referred to above regarding our Savior's conflict with the enemy in the wilderness proves to be a sitting illustration of this designation. On one hand the enemy used the same word of scripture to throw an offense against our Savior, and our Savior used the same word of scripture to defend the integrity of scripture. Further, in this wilderness conflict another great lesson is left on record for us as believers. **Note:** this battle was nothing more than a spiritual battle. It was a battle over words. The only sword that Jesus had was the word of God. As a matter-of-fact inspiration pointed to a time in Revelation 12, that there was a war in heaven, and we are told that the instruments, the articles of war, weaponry, was nothing else but the word. It was the word of God against the word of the adversary. And as always, the word—which is truth—holds sway over any and all lies. Thus truth is stronger than error. It is for this reason that the Savior says in St. John 17:17, *"Sanctify them through thy truth: thy word is* *truth."* The word and truth is inseparable. For us as believers, error cannot exist on its own, it has to attach itself to the truth. This powerful weapon is able to discern; *"For the word of God is quick, and powerful, and sharper than any two-edged sword, piercing even to the dividing asunder of soul and spirit, and of the joints and marrow, and is a discerner of the thoughts and intents of the heart."* Hebrews 4:12.

Enduring Affliction Builds Godly Character
Section III

Section III

Enduring Affliction Builds Godly Character

Endurance

The dictionary defines endurance as: *To hold out against; sustain without impairment or yielding; undergo: to bear without resistance; to suffer patiently; to tolerate: To continue or carry on despite obstacles or hardships. To remain firm, as under trial or suffering; to bear up under adversity.*

In those moments of temptations and the enemy's suggestion to ask and to inquire as to why this is happening to me, in those very moments, we ought to be reminded of the Apostle Peter's encouraging admonition, *"Beloved, think it not strange concerning the fiery trial which is to try you, as though some strange thing happened unto you:"* -I Peter 4:12. It is with this same thought that the Apostle James buttresses Peter's statement by adding, *"My brethren, count it all joy when ye fall into divers temptations, knowing that the trying of your faith worketh patience."* James 1:2-3.

Endurance then, is an essential, must-have, sterling, christian trait. Endurance serves to separate the true sons of God from those who merely profess to be believers. Endurance is a distinguishing mark, yes even the mark of demarcation between those who serve the Lord and those who serve Him not. Endurance is not an option. Endurance is not a suggestion, nay endurance is a command, and this command was given and exhibited in the lives of every true follower of Christ today. There is only one path to victory for the believer and that path is the path of endurance paved with the "stones" of affliction.

One of the key benefits of enduring is maturing. Patient endurance when tested, brings the believer into divine alignment with God's plans and purposes. It stabilizes your faith walk; for it is through faith that one endures with success. I Peter 5:10 declares, *"But the God of all grace, who hath called us unto His eternal glory by Christ Jesus, after that ye have suffered a while, make you perfect, stablish, strengthen, settle you."*

Many believers today crumble under pressure, not realizing that it has been designed to arouse and bring forth the sweet aroma of God's glory in and from their lives. When this aroma begins to emanate, you will effectively begin to impact the lives of others. The believer must patiently endure, with the understanding that a promise awaits at the end of each test; therefore, standing firm in faith while experiencing trials has great value. There are times you may seek answers or help, because of the severity of the trial, but to no avail. It is often because God is working on the inside of you to make you a prototype of Himself. He knows the right timing to answer, to give aid, to manifest, to release, to deliver and liberate you. *"He hath made everything beautiful in His time:"* Ecclesiastes 3:11. It is for your perfection.

The Apostle Paul counsels the believer to persist in the midst of hardship. *"Thou therefore endure hardness as a good soldier of Jesus Christ."* II Timothy 2:3. Endurance is power. It invigorates maturity.

Affliction

According to the dictionary, the word affliction derives directly from the Latin word, *afflictionem*, which means to damage, harass, distress, torment.

The Psalmist says in Psalm 34:19, "Many are the afflictions of the righteous; but the Lord delivereth him out of them all." The word of God clears all doubt that affliction and trials are but a necessary path of the believer's experience. The world in which we live is filled with turbulence and the believer is not exempt in any way from life's various avenues of afflictions. Let it not be once thought or even imagined that turbulence and affliction comes as a result of wrongdoing or of spiritual impropriety. It can be said that affliction was fashioned to propel you into the presence of the Lord, therefore it is intentional.

You must endeavor to progress through the pain. Why? Because out of it comes forth perfection, refinement, beauty and godliness. Affliction has a significant purpose; so the question may be asked, what is the spiritual significance of affliction, and why is it that heaven has ordained it to be a part of our growth experience? **It is because it defines who you truly are.** Though it is weighty, and sometimes may seem unbearable, it is necessary to the fulfillment of your God-given purpose, therefore, it should be viewed as a good thing because greatness emerges from it.

Let us take a look at the life of Joseph; he was gravely hated by his brothers who threw him into a waterless pit and left him to die. Shortly thereafter, they sold him to the Ishmaelites for twenty pieces of silver, who in turn sold him to Potiphar in Egypt. Potiphar's wife falsely accused him of sexual harassment and had him thrown into prison. He was totally forgotten by the chief butler who had promised to help him. Despite his great affliction, he stayed the course and God was with him. Joseph understood that his purpose was greater than his pain, so he endured the fiery trials. At the end, he was promoted to the office of the Prime Minister of Egypt (Chief Executive Officer).

Afflictions have many components which can be oppressive and distressing. It can give off a sense of rejection, causing the believer to disconnect from others. It can drive you to a place of loneliness and dysfunction; and if you're not careful, it can strip you of exuberance, causing bitterness and resentment. Afflictions can cause the believer to become poisonous, spiteful and revengeful, hence spewing venom. But despite all of its components, it has not been designed to destroy you. The believer must know that in order to mature (develop) on this spiritual journey, affliction is necessary. Therefore, you must prepare your mind, heart and spirit to embrace this element of suffering which has been designed as an avenue to catapult you into your divine calling and destiny.

Affliction is in comparison to being on the potter's wheel. It should never be aborted but should be allowed to thrust the child of God into a disciplined lifestyle of prayer and fasting, word intake and application, praise and inspiration for the purpose of godliness.

The Scriptures tells us in Malachi 3:2-3, *"For he is like a refiner's fire and fullers' soap: and he shall sit as a refiner and purifier of silver: and he shall purify the sons of Levi, and purge them as gold and silver, that they may offer unto the Lord an offering in righteousness."* This furnace of affliction is heaven ordained and none other than God Himself is the overseer of the refining process. We are therefore assured the fiery process is not to destroy the believer but rather to purify him, thus making him a vessel of honor. Fire then is the most complete and powerful cleansing, purifying agent, even as we see it in a temporal setting.

Little wonder that the Psalmist under inspiration states emphatically, "many are the afflictions of the righteous; but the Lord delivereth him out of them all." It's important to note that the afflictions are "ours" but the deliverance comes from the Lord. In other words our lot is to endure afflictions/hardness; His lot is to deliver/save. This is nothing less than a supernatural, highly spiritual, symbiotic relationship.

Let us hear the conclusion of the matter, our Savior says to each and every one of us, "He that endureth to the end, the same shall be saved." Matthew 24:13. The believer then has this assurance, based on the testimony of God's own words, that as for afflictions, "affliction should not rise up a second time." Nahum 1:9.

Character

The word character is a developing process of moral strength or qualities; integrity, personality and uniqueness makes up the sum-total of the individual.

The prophet Malachi said in chapter 3:1, *"For I am the Lord, I change not."* Hebrews 13:8 states, *"Jesus Christ is the same yesterday and today and forever."* These two scriptural references point to the immutable character of God, and as such, He requires we have His character perfectly reproduced within each of us.

Dr. Myles Munroe puts it this way, "it is the dedication to a set of standards without wavering." "It is a self-impose discipline for the sake of moral conviction." "Character is a protector of your words, your deeds and your actions; it's a constant effort to integrate them as one." "Character is unchanging."

The believer's character is of greater significance to God, than the afflictions they undergo; or even the gifts and talents they are graced with.

There are times, the believer's life experiences become traumatic; but in the midst of this testing period, the believer must learn to patiently wait on, and trust God, allowing Him to scale off the old wineskin so that there be an emergence of the new. There must be a deep penetration of God's Word in the heart, mind and spirit of the believer in order for this transformation to take place.

In Ephesians 4:22-24, the Apostle Paul strongly admonishes the child of God, *"That ye put off concerning the former conversation, the old man which is corrupt according to the deceitful lusts; And be renewed in the spirit of your mind; And that ye put on the new man, which after God is created in righteousness and true holiness."* Adorning oneself with this new wineskin is absolutely required. This processing or developing of godly character is not instant, nor is it easy; but He has already given unto the believer everything that pertains to life and godliness to enable the believer to mirror their heavenly Father. In other words, the seed of the un-altering, changeless, eternal Word of life has been planted within the hearts and spirits of the believer, so that the believer can grow, mature, advance, elevate, and birth forth the character and attributes of God. God's word is a reflection of His character.

It bears repeating, character building is not an instantaneous achievement, but rather it is a work of a lifetime. In other words, character and sanctification are interchangeable. Neither can be bought at the local pharmacy or supermarket, it is left to the individual to strive and attain perfection in Christ. The early Presbyterian believers taught and preached that the only thing one can take from earth to glory is character. The nucleus of God's character is love and His very nature is holiness. His color is light and in Him, there is no darkness at all. Darkness represents sin, evil and wicked works, but "Love," "Holiness" and "Light" is His Person; they represent who He truly is. Hannah's response to her circumstances exemplified the very character of God.

We read in the book of Job, how his character was developed after being tested to the very core. The trials (afflictions) he experienced were weighty. He lost everything including his sons and daughters who were dear to his heart, his health declined tremendously, and his wife asked him to curse God and die. Even in this we are amazed at Job's responses. Hear the patriarch, *"Though he slay me, yet will I trust Him: but I will maintain mine own ways before Him."* -Job 13:15. Later down in his discourse the aged servant of God said, *"but he knoweth the way that I take: when he hath tried me, I shall come forth as gold."* Further, he continued to declare his position as he says, *"God forbid that I should justify you: till I die I will not remove mine integrity from me."* Job 27:5. And then as if to seal and stamp the state of his character, *"Let me be weighed in an even balance that God may know mine integrity."* Job 31:6.

Despite Job's painful afflictions, he maintained his character; he never accused God foolishly. To every son of God, we must often be reminded that your reputation is what your fellow man and fellow believer say about you, but your character is what (the people who are intimate with you) your wife and children know about you. Character then is the sum-total of the man, his thoughts, his words, his impulses, his passions, his decisions are all governed by and under the spirit of truth.

Wisdom Nuggets for Daily Devotions

Section IV

Day 1

Always persevere in doing
that which is good and right.

"And let us not grow weary in well doing, for in due season we shall reap, if we faint not." -Galatians 6:9

One must with great determination remain constant even in the face of adversity.

PERSEVERANCE IN ESSENCE IS TO STAY THE COURSE.

Day 2

Embrace every opportunity to
walk humbly before God.

"Humble yourselves in the sight of the Lord, and he shall lift you up."
- James 4:10.

Hannah's attitude of humility invoked God's attention.
A humble child tastes the grace of God.

HUMILITY IS A SUPREME TEST OF CHARACTER.

Day 3

Active faith coupled with hard work determines success

"Seest thou how faith wrought with his works, and by works was faith made perfect?" –James 2:22

Hannah's faith/work equaled victory.

FAITH INTERTWINED WITH WORK PRODUCES LASTING RESULTS.

Day 4

Be resolved in releasing quickly the assaults of others

"Take heed to yourselves: if your brother trespass against you, rebuke him; and if he repents, forgive him. And if he trespass against you seven times in a day, and seven times in a day turn again to you, saying, I repent; you shall forgive him."
Luke 17:3-4

Forgive instantly, embrace immeasurable peace and live free.

DELAYED FORGIVENESS DETERIORATES SPIRITUAL HEALTH, HENCE IT DETERIORATES LIFE.

Day 5

Walking in offense cripples your walk in the spirit

He that saith he abideth in him ought himself also so to walk, even as he walked." I John 2:6

Offense is nothing more than an antithesis to the law of God.

OFFENSE ALSO REVEALS ONE'S LACK OF LOVE FOR GOD'S LAW.

Day 6

Yesterday's inspiration is insufficient to attain Christian victory today

"While it is said, Today if ye will hear his voice, harden not your hearts, as in the provocation." Hebrews 3:15

Trying to carry out today's task with yesterday's instructions is suicidal. Yesterday's home-run is no guarantee of victory in today's game of life.

SUFFICIENT UNTO THE DAY IS THE EVIL THEREFORE.

Day 7

Allow your thoughts and actions to daily resemble that of Christ's.

"Let this mind be in you, which was also in Christ Jesus."
-Philippians 2:5

God's greatest desire is for man to become like Him.

HANNAH MIRRORED HER HEAVENLY FATHER.

Day 8

Indulge daily in God's word for spiritual growth and advancement.

"But his delight is in the law of the Lord; and in His law doth he meditate day and night. And he shall be like a tree planted by the rivers of water, that bringeth forth its fruit in his season," -Psalm 1:2-3

In-taking the Word daily is your heavenly sustenance.

THE WORD OF GOD WILL EITHER MAKE OR BREAK YOU; BLESS OR BLISTER YOU.

Day 9

Remain steadfast when faced
with adverse circumstances.

"We are troubled on every side, yet not distressed; we are perplexed, but not in despair; persecuted, but not forsaken; cast down, but not destroyed;"
-*II Corinthians 4:8-9*

Hannah stood undaunted in the midst of life's crisis.

ADVERSITIES INTENTION GIVES BIRTH TO PROMOTION.

Day 10

Hold fast to the promises of God without wavering

"For all the promises of God in Him are "Yea," and in Him 'Amen," unto the glory of God by us." -II Corinthians 1:20.

Swaying between doubt and belief—by default—renders one incapable of receiving the blessings of God.

HIS PROMISES STILL STAND!

.

Day 11

Allow progression to be the theme of your life

"I press toward the mark for the prize of the high calling of God in Christ Jesus."
-Philippians 3:14

The christian march should be ever onward, forward, upward unto the high calling which is in Jesus our Lord.

IN THIS LIFE WE ARE EITHER PROGRESSING CLOSER TOWARD GOD OR REGRESSING AWAY FROM GOD.

Day 12

Always remember that your life is
an open book being read by others.

"Ye are our epistles written in our hearts, known and read of all men."
-II Corinthians 3:2

The sermon of your life is not heard but seen.

YOUR LIFE IS NOT MARKED BY THE TITLE YOU WEAR, BUT BY THAT WHICH EMANATES FROM WITHIN.

.

Day 13

Keep your spiritual pipeline freed
from that which defiles.

"And he said, that which cometh out of the man, that defileth the man. For from within, out of the heart of men, proceed evil thoughts..."
–Mark 7:20 – 21a.

Thrive daily to safeguard the purity of your heart.

A SEPTIC HEART IS DESTRUCTIVE AND SULLLIES HEALTHY RELATIONSHIPS.

Day 14

Guard well the thought patterns of your mind.

"Finally brethren, whatsoever things are true, whatsoever things are honest, whatsoever things are just, whatsoever things are pure, whatsoever things are lovely, whatsoever things are of good report, if there be any virtue, and if there be any praise, think on these things." –Philippians 4:8

A renewed mind brings freedom and causes you to manifest what is that good, and acceptable and perfect will of God.

YOUR THOUGHTS ARE THE VEHICLE THAT TAKES YOU TO YOUR DESTINY.

Day 15

Never withhold compassion from others.

Never withhold compassion from others.
"But whoso hath this world's good, and seeth his brother have need, and shutteth up his bowels of compassion from him, how dwelleth the love of God in him?"
– I John 3:17.

The engine of love moves the believer to true compassion.

COMPASSION IS THE EMBODIMENT OF AGAPE LOVE.

Day 16

Character construction is the most necessary discipline for godly living

"But I keep under my body, and bring it into subjection: lest that by any means, when I have preached to others, I myself should be a castaway."
-I Corinthians" 9:27.

To obtain a life of holiness requires more than chance.

GODLY LIVING AND HOLINESS ARE SYNONYMOUS. CONSTRUCTING A GODLY CHARACTER REQUIRES MORE THAN JUST HAPPENSTANCE. IT IS PURPOSEFUL.

Day 17

Consistency is a pathway to complete triumph over the enemy.

"Seest thou a man diligent in his business? He shall stand before kings, he shall not stand before mean men." -Proverbs 22:29

In business, an industrious person equals a successful individual.

WHATEVER YOUR HAND FIND TO DO, DO IT WITH ALL YOUR MIGHT.

Day 18

Determination not desire controls your destiny.

"When she had heard of Jesus, came in the press behind, and touched his garment. For she said, if I may touch but his clothes, I shall be whole."

–Mark 5:27-28

Persistency is being far more than a desire, but is sheer determination.

PERSISTENCY COURTS THE VERY PRESENCE OF GOD.

Day 19

Never allow the vicissitudes of life to paralyze your relationship with God.

"Who shall separate us from the love of Christ?"

–Romans 8:35

True commitment supersedes more than just casual involvement but rather total dedication and complete sacrifice.

HOLD FAST TO GOD UNCHANGING HANDS.

Day 20

View others through the eyes of God.

"And he turned to the woman, and said unto Simon, Seest thou this woman?" -Luke 7:44

"And shall make him of quick understanding in fear of the Lord: and he shall not judge after the sight of his eyes." -Isaiah 11:3.

Do not look at individuals based on their past failures.

ASK GOD TO LET YOU SEE THEM THROUGH THE LENS OF HIS MERCY.

Day 21

Itinerant your life according to God's divine will.

"So teach us to number our days, that we may apply our hearts unto wisdom."
–Psalm 90:12.

When you are spiritually conscious of time, your life becomes productive.

EVERY NANO SECOND YOU HAVE IS A GIFT FROM GOD.

Day 22

He who searches out wisdom
shall be greatly rewarded.

"So shall the knowledge of wisdom be unto thy soul: when thou hast found it, then there shall be a reward, and thy expectation shall not be cut off."
–Proverbs 24:14.

Wise decisions bring high productivity;
but decisions void of wisdom prove to be fatal.

**WISDOM BEING SOUGHT ABOVE ALL ELSE
PAYS OFF HANDSOMELY.**

Day 23

Righteous living cannot be achieved through self-efforts.

"*In righteousness shalt thou be established:*" Isaiah 54:14a.

Daily application of the word of God intimately

contributes to living

an upright life.

HE DEEPLY ROOTS US IN HIMSELF; THEREFORE, RIGHTEOUSNESS IS NOT EARNED, IT IS A GIFT FROM GOD.

Day 24

You were effectively advancing, what doth hinder you now?

"Remember therefore from whence thou art fallen, and repent, and do the first works; or else I will come unto thee quickly, and will remove thy candlestick out of his place, except thou repent." –Revelation 2:5.

Somewhere along your journey, you got distracted, your gifts became dormant and your love has turned cold.

YOU DON'T LOVE ME LIKE YOU USE TO, REPENT AND ALLOW ME TO REKINDLE MY FIRE WITHIN YOU ONCE MORE.

Day 25

Trust God,
His timing is not your timing.

"All the days of my appointed time will I wait, till my change."
- Job 14:14b.

God's moving ability is not based on a clock or time.

HE DIVINELY MANEUVERS BEHIND THE SCENES.

Day 26

Kingdom-minded people are not time wasters but are wise managers of time and opportunities.

"See then that ye walk circumspectly, not as fools, but as wise; Redeeming the time, because the days are evil." Ephesians 5:15-16.

We ourselves are the arbiters of the events into which we come into contact, as we travel the pathway of time that leads to eternity .

ELIMINATE TIME WASTERS AND USE YOUR TIME WITH ABSOLUTE CARE.

Day 27

God's Word is but a reflection of His integrity.

"God is not a man that he should lie; neither the son of man, that he should repent:" Numbers 23:19.

"For he spake, and it was done; he commanded, and it stood fast." Psalm 33:9

All of His commandments are faithful and His words are forever settled in heaven.

GREAT IS HIS FAITHFULNESS!

Day 28

Strive to live a productive and fruitful life.

"Ye have not chosen me, but I have chosen you, and ordained you. That ye should go and bring forth fruit, and that your fruit should remain:" -John 15:16.

Always aim toward producing peaceable fruits of righteousness.

A FRUIT BEARING BELIEVER BRINGS GLORY AND HONOUR TO OUR HEAVENLY FATHER.

Day 29

Never allow your physical condition to dictate your spiritual position.

"And at midnight Paul and Silas prayed, and sang praises unto God: and the prisoners heard them. And suddenly there was such a great earthquake, so that the foundations of the prison were shaken: And immediately all the doors opened, and every one's bands were loosed." -Acts. 16:25-26.

You must remain seated with God in a heavenly place despite your circumstances.

THE PRISON'S DUNGEON, THOUGH DEGRADING AND DISCOURAGING, WAS NOT DEVASTATING ENOUGH TO REMOVE PAUL AND SILAS OUT OF THEIR SPIRITUAL POSTURE.

Day 30

Never be moved by what others think or say about your past life-style.

'There is therefore now no condemnation to them which are in Christ Jesus, who walk not after the flesh, but after the Spirit."
–Romans 8:1.

Even if your heart condemns you, God is greater than your heart.

BE CONFIDENT IN WHO YOU ARE AND WHOSE YOU ARE AT ALL TIMES.

Day 31

Never let your left hand know what your right hand is doing.

"Give not that which is holy unto the dogs, neither cast ye your pearls before swine, lest they trample them under their feet, and turn again and rend you."
–Matthew 7:6

Be careful in releasing information to the wrong source.

THAT REQUIRES THE WISDOM OF SOLOMON, THE PATIENCE OF JOB AND THE LOVE OF THE APOSTLE PAUL.

QUESTIONS FOR SELF-EVALUATION
(Answer in your spare time.)

Do you involve God in your moment to moment, day-to-day activities? _____ If *yes*, How? If *no*, Why not?

_____
_____
_____
_____
_____

Have you set goals for your life? _____.

    a) Describe what they are._____

_____
_____
_____
_____
_____

    b) How do you plan to accomplish them? _____

_____
_____
_____
_____
_____

How are you representing Christ on earth?_____

_____
_____
_____
_____

P.R.A.Y.E.R

Gives you:

POWER over the agencies of the enemy. (principalities/ wickedness in high places/rulers of darkness).

RESTORES you back into a right relationship with God and others.

AFFIRMS who God is in your life.

Gives you a:
YEARNING to please Him.

Causes you to be:
EFFECTIVE in annihilating demonic systems.

REJUVENATES the physical and spiritual man.

PRAYER MAKES EVERYTHING ELSE POSSIBLE
(More things are wrought by prayer than this world dreams of.)
by Alfred Tennyson.

ABOUT THE AUTHOR

Dorothy V. McIntosh was born in Abaco, Bahamas. She is the ninth child in a family of eleven children. She dedicates much of her time to prayer and is used by God in the areas of healing, deliverance, and prophetic intercession. Her life's mission is to establish a refuge for hurting women and provide them with the ministries necessary for healing and restoration.

She is an author, teacher, preacher, visionary, prayer warrior, and songwriter, in addition to being a loving mother, grandmother, and friend

Dorothy has a deep love and passion for God and His work. She is an ordained Pastor, and Founder of "The Prayer Room Ministry," an Apostolic and Prophetic Prayer House, and is the CEO of "Apostolic Team Ministry" ATM.

www.ingramcontent.com/pod-product-compliance
Lightning Source LLC
Chambersburg PA
CBHW030347100526
44592CB00010B/856